THINGS
That Swim
In Texas Waters*
ALPHABETICALLY SPEAKING

Text by Glenna Grimmer
Photographs by H. Dickson Hoese

* **And in other coastal states of
the Gulf of Mexico**

With special thanks to:

George Grimmer III, whose bright mind and spirit delights us all.

Dr. H. Dickson Hoese of the University of Southwestern Louisiana, without whose knowledge, patience, and slides this book would not have been possible.

Bob Snow of Snow Graphic Designs, Carrollton, Texas, for his cover design and drawings.

Friends and nature lovers whose interest in my other books has encouraged me to write this one.

OTHER BOOKS BY GLENNA GRIMMER

The ABCs of Texas Wildflowers
Texas Birds from A to Z

FIRST EDITION

Copyright © 1989
By Glenna Grimmer

Published in the United States of America
By Eakin Press, P.O. Drawer 90159, Austin, Texas 78709-0159

ISBN 0-89015-694-8

Library of Congress Cataloging-in-Publication Data

Grimmer, Glenna, 1924–
    Things that swim in Texas waters* alphabetically speaking : *and in other Coastal States of the Gulf of Mexico / by Glenna Grimmer : photographs by H. Dickson Hoese.
        p.   cm.
    Bibliography: p.
    Summary: Discusses twenty-six animals who inhabit the lakes, rivers, and Gulf waters of Texas and other coastal states of the Gulf of Mexico, arranged alphabetically from Alligator to Zosterae.
    ISBN 0-89015-694-8 : $11.95
    1. Aquatic animals — Texas — Dictionaries. Juvenile. 2. Aquatic animals — Gulf States — Dictionaries, Juvenile. [1. Aquatic animals — Texas — Dictionaries. 2. Aquatic animals — Gulf States — Dictionaries.] I. Hoese, H. Dickson, ill. II. Title.
QL207.C75   1989
596'.09276 — dc19
                                     88-37533
                                         CIP
                                         AC

Contents

"Rainy-Day Fishing"

I sat by the window watching it rain —
I was visiting at Grandpa's house again.

He promised we'd go fishing down at the creek,
We'd been planning the trip for most of the week.

And now it was raining and I was real mad
But Grandpa said there was no need to be sad.

Grandpa said instead of just wishing
He'd show me a new kind of way to go fishing.

"We don't need a pole or even a hook,
We'll do our fishing right out of a book."

Grandpa likes to teach me things
All about bugs and bees that sting.

He knows all about the birds that fly
And about the stars way up in the sky.

I looked at the book in front of him;
It told all about the things that swim.

"We'll start with A and go to Z
We'll learn about fish alphabetically."

We had a hard time with some of the letters,
But Grandpa said that made the game better.

He put all the names into a song;
I didn't know the words so I hummed along.

The next time he sang it all the way through
I was able to name the swimming things too.

— Glenna Grimmer

Introduction

Did you ever stop to think about all the creatures that spend their entire lives in the water? There are so many that a person could spend a lifetime studying them and never reach the end of the long, long list.

If you like to swim, just imagine what it would be like to live in the water all the time. Because we were meant to live on dry land, we couldn't live in the water. Very soon our skin would shrivel and we would resemble prunes. And we couldn't stay under water for very long without breathing.

But for *aquatic* animals, this is a natural way of life. Because approximately seven-tenths of the earth's surface is made up of water, there are many, many more creatures that live in the water than live out of it. Some of them are so small that they have to be viewed under a microscope, or they may be so large that the waves they make can rock a large ship.

We usually think of things that live in the water as "fish," most of which have *gills, scales,* and *fins.* There are many different and unusual kinds of fish. But, as you will discover, there are also other creatures that live in the water.

To study all the fish and *amphibians* in the United States would fill up many volumes, so we are going to study only those found in Texas waters — rivers, lakes, streams, ponds, and the Gulf of Mexico. Even that number would be much too great for one book, so we are going to cover an alphabet of things that swim in Texas waters. Although the book is written about Texas creatures, all of them are found in many other places. Some are found worldwide, some in the eastern and southeastern United States. Generally speaking, most aquatic animals that are found in Texas are also found in the waters of other Gulf states: Louisiana, Mississippi, Alabama, and Florida.

Some of the creatures in this book are classified as fish, some are amphibians, one is a mammal, but they are all animals. We have selected twenty-six, one for each letter of the alphabet.

It was difficult to find an average size for each one because a creature may continue to grow throughout its lifetime and its growth may slow down as it ages. We have given the average weights and lengths of fully grown or adult animals. As you will see, some of the animals are very light in weight while others are very heavy. Our photographer and consultant, Dr. H. Dickson Hoese of the University of Southwestern Louisiana, says that it was a challenge to find weights for every letter of our alphabet. Weights for many "things" such as the newt, jellyfish, and sea urchin could not be found in printed texts. We appreciate the fact that Dr. Hoese and his staff weighed these creatures so the information could be included in our book.

If you do not find your favorite fish or aquatic animal listed, start your own alphabet and see how many you can find for each letter. This book is only a beginning. We hope it will encourage you to go further in your study.

All animals, plants, fish, and birds have two kinds of names: a *scientific name,* which is usually hard to pronounce, and a common name, which is like a nickname. In this book, we have used the common names in our alphabet except for "I," "X," and "Z." We have also given scientific names to show the difference. As you study further, you will want to know more about the scientific names because they can help with identification. Scientific names are always in *italics.* The first word, which is the *genus* name, always begins with a capital letter. The second word, which is the *species* name, begins with a lowercase letter.

Common names may vary from place to place, and whenever possible, we have given several common names by which a particular animal is known. Fish and amphibians, like other living things, belong to families. Classifications of families can be very technical and difficult to do. However, we have included family names when possible. For example, there are several spearfish families. The volador belongs to one of them. Also, the hardhead catfish belongs to a catfish family, but there are several such family groupings.

The plural forms of creature names can also be confusing. For instance, the word "fish" can mean one or more than one. You can also make fish plural by adding "es," or "fishes." Either form is correct. More than one octopus can be octopuses or octopi. Although this may seem confusing, it can also be challenging. Check a dictionary to add to your knowledge about things that live in the water.

Ichthyology is a hard-to-pronounce word that means the study of fish. *Zoology* means the study of all animals. Although most of our alphabet are fish, some belong to other classifications.

As you read, you will notice that some of the words that are not scientific names are also in *italics*. Because these *italicized* words may be new to you, we have put them into a glossary in the back of the book.

At the beginning of the book, you will find a song, "Singing About Things Alphabetically." This song will help you learn the name that goes with each letter of the alphabet. The tune for the song is a very old one called "Skip to My Lou." If you don't know it, I'm sure your parents or grandparents can help you learn it. Singing is a fun way to learn.

When you have explored this book, you may want to read others. We have included a bibliography, which may help you with further reading.

If you like to go fishing, take the book along and see if any of the fish you catch match one from our alphabet. Whether you fish or not, whether you live by the water or miles inland, it's always fun to learn something new. *Things That Swim in Texas Waters, Alphabetically Speaking* was written to help you explore the waters of Texas. Have fun with it.

"Singing About Things Alphabetically"
(Sing to "Skip to My Lou")

Can't go fishing on a rainy day
But we can be cheerful anyway
Naming things from A to Z
That swim in Texas waters.

Why don't you sing along with me?
We'll have fun just wait and see
Naming things alphabetically
That swim in Texas waters.

Alligator, bass, crab, and drum
Eel, flounder, gar's another one
Hardhead, *Isurus** is a name for a shark
That swims in Texas waters.

Jellyfish, killifish, and one named ling
We can be learning as we sing.
Mullet, newt, octopus, and porpoise
All swim in Texas waters.

Queen angel, ribbonfish, and stingaree
Turtle, urchin in the bottom of the sea;
The Spanish call one volador
That swims in Texas waters.

Whiting, *Xiphias** must do for "X"
Yellowfin is the one that's next
And last there is a *zosterae**
That swims in Texas waters.

Now we've found our alphabet
Sing it again so you won't forget
Naming things from A to Z
That swim in Texas waters.

Why don't you sing along with me?
We'll have fun just wait and see.
Singing about things alphabetically
That swim in Texas waters.

— Glenna Grimmer

*Scientific names

7

ALLIGATOR, American

Scientific Name:	*Alligator mississippiensis*
Other Names:	Gator, el lagarto (Spanish), cocodrie (Louisiana)
Average Weight:	500 pounds
Average Length:	6–15 feet
Texas Habitat:	Freshwater, *brackish* marshes, swamps, rivers, and bayous along the southeast coast of Texas

Once you've seen an alligator, you're not likely to forget it. Not only is this the largest *reptile* in North America, it is also the loudest.

American alligators are common in the coastal waters of southeast Texas, but they are not found in the central or western parts of the United States. They are often seen sleeping at water's edge or in their habitat at the zoo, but it is best not to get too close to an alligator. They appear to be slow moving, but when aroused, they can move quickly. The alligator will open and close its large, long *snout* (which holds eighty or ninety sharp teeth) or swing its long, powerful tail to strike its prey. So many alligators have been killed for their hides that they are now protected by the Endangered Species Act.

The male alligator has a very loud, lusty bellow — especially during the spring mating season. After mating, the female builds a nest-ing mound near or in water. Then she lays twenty to sixty eggs and covers them with veg-etation. She stays near the eggs until they hatch ten weeks later. The female may stay with her young for as long as two years. Just hatched alligators are about ten inches long. Young alligators eat small frogs, *crustaceans,* and aquatic insects. The adults eat turtles, birds, fish, blue crabs, crayfish, and small mammals.

American alligators have broad, rounded, somewhat flat snouts; their long tails taper to a point with a high crest of scales. The body is covered with rough scales on the back, but the belly is smooth. Old adults are gray-black; im-mature alligators are black with yellow cross bands. Alligators have raised nostrils and popped eyes, which enables them to swim just beneath the surface of the water without get-ting their noses or eyes wet.

BASS, largemouth

Scientific Name: *Micropterus salmoides*
Other Names: Black bass, bigmouth bass, green trout
Average Weight: 2 to 6 pounds, but a 10-pound largemouth is not unusual
Average Length: 1½–24 inches
Texas Habitat: All freshwater lakes, ponds, and rivers throughout the state

The largemouth bass is a favorite freshwater fish among Texas fishermen. Although it is called a "bass," it actually belongs to the Sunfish Family and is the largest member of that family. It is a *native* fish. Because it has been raised in fish *hatcheries* for more than fifty years and distributed throughout the state, it may be found in thousands of lakes and ponds in Texas.

The largemouth bass *spawns* in Texas in spring when the water temperatures are nearly sixty degrees. The male largemouth uses his tail to fan out a nest and then attracts a female to it. The nest is usually in quiet waters, at depths of two to eight feet.

A female largemouth bass may lay as many as 2,000 to 25,000 eggs, which are quickly *fertilized* by the male. The female is then driven away and the male watches over the *incubating* eggs. To keep the eggs from suffocating, the male moves his fins back and forth, causing the water to continually circulate over the eggs. The young fish, which are called *fry,* hatch in five to ten days and stay close together in a school. For several more days, the male fish continues to guard them and provide food.

When the young largemouth are two inches long, they become little *predators* and will eat almost anything they can catch.

Largemouth bass may reach a length of twelve to fourteen inches and weigh one pound by the end of the first year. They usually live for six to eight years, but they may live even longer than that in a protected environment.

Largemouth bass are green on the top of their bodies and have dark, *mottled* blotches along the sides. These blend into dark stripes. The underside of this fish is a lighter shade.

CRAB, blue

Scientific Name: *Callinectes sapidus*
Average Weight: **1/4–1/2 pound**
Average Length: **3–7 inches**
Texas Habitat: *Bays, estuaries,* **offshore waters**

The blue crab is one of the most common *crustaceans* in Texas. It is also one of the most highly prized as a food source.

The *carapace,* or shell, of a blue crab is bluish-green and oval-shaped. The blue crab is easy to identify because it is the only one with sharp spikes along the side of its shell. The blue crab is twice as wide from side to side as it is from front to back. The legs of this crab are blue except for those that end in claws, which are also called *pincers.* The pincers are a reddish-brown and look like a pair of sharp, curved pliers.

Crabs are among the most interesting crustaceans, not only because of the way they look but because of their habits and body structure. The eyes of the blue crab stand out on short stalks, and there are four teeth between the eyes. Because the crab has ten pairs of legs, it is

also called a *decapod.* The legs are adapted for walking or swimming, except for those with pincers. These are used for grabbing food and for protection. Although crabs usually move sideways, they can move in any direction.

Crabs, like other crustaceans, *molt.* At this time they are in danger of becoming food for larger creatures. Like other crustaceans, they have jointed legs and two pairs of *antennae.*

Male crabs fertilize the eggs of the female after the female molts. A female may produce as many as one to five million eggs. Females are said to be *berried* when they are carrying their eggs. They may be found throughout most of the year, but the peak of the breeding season is June and July.

The blue crab prefers to live on the bottom of shallow, muddy water. This crab belongs to the Swimming Crab Family.

DRUM, black

Scientific Name:	*Pogonias cromis*
Other Names:	**Drum fish, Texas drum, sea drum, gray drum, drumfish, banded drum**
Average Weight:	**30 pounds (young black drum will average 4–5 pounds)**
Average Length:	**6–36 inches**
Texas Habitat:	**Sandy bays, inland waters, and all coastal waters**

Young black drums are easy to recognize because of the four or five dark, vertical bars or bands. These bars become less noticeable as the fish ages, giving it a more uniform, dark color. Black drums have *barbels,* or short whiskers, hanging from under their chins. They have a divided *dorsal fin* and a short *anal fin,* both of which are dark in color.

This is the largest member of the Drum Family. The fish feeds along the bottom and has a special taste for shrimp, crab, and small oysters. It also eats some fish. Because of its appetite, the black drum is not popular with commercial crabbers, shrimpers, or oystermen. However, it is itself a good, edible fish.

Black drums are raised and sold commercially. They are also caught on hooks and lines by fishermen. Catching a black drum is not as exciting as catching a red drum, which is considered a *game fish.*

The Drum Family gets its name from the "drumming" sounds its members make. The sounds are caused by *contracting* muscles near the *swim bladder.* The black drum, as the largest member of this family, can make the loudest noise.

11

EEL, spotted moray

Scientific Name: *Gymnothoray moringa*
Average Weight: 5 pounds
Average Length: 3 feet
Texas Habitat: *Subtropical* waters of the Texas coast; offshore coral *reefs* and rocky areas

Moray eels have thick, leathery skin and flattened bodies. Their gill openings are small and round, their teeth large and sharp, and their jaws strong.

There are more than eighty species of morays, but only a few of them venture into Texas waters. Most morays are large, reaching a length of five to six feet, but some are as long as twenty feet; a few are less than six inches long. The eel pictured in this book is a spotted moray and is one of the smaller species. It is called "spotted" because it has a brown or blackish speckled pattern on a white to yellow background.

The moray has an unusual way of capturing its prey. Putting the rear half of its body into a crevice or hole, its front half is free to swing around toward the prey. With mouth open and freedom of movement, the moray is ready to capture whatever comes close.

Although not considered dangerous if left undisturbed, morays will attack anything, including divers, if they feel cornered or caught. In spite of what many people believe, eel bites are not poisonous. But a large eel can leave an ugly, jagged wound that can easily get infected and is often slow to heal. All morays should be handled with care if they must be handled at all.

Most morays are *nocturnal* creatures. They are always looking for a meal and will grab one whenever they can. Moray eels are considered edible in many parts of the world, but they are not a very popular dish in Texas.

Other species of the Moray Family found in Texas include the green moray, purplemouth moray, and ocellated moray, which is often caught in nets by shrimpers.

FROG, southern leopard

Scientific Name: *Rana utricularia*
Average Weight: 3¹/₂ ounces
Average Length: 2–9 inches
Texas Habitat: Shallow freshwater and slightly brackish marshes over most of East Texas

The southern leopard frog is green or brown with dark spots. It has a slender head, pointed snout, and light-colored ridges. This particular species is found in East Texas, but several other species of leopard frogs which are very similar occur in other parts of Texas.

Frogs are typical amphibians, beginning their life in the water as *tadpoles* with tails. As the tadpoles grow, the tails disappear and they develop legs. They can then live either in water or on land, though much of their life is spent on the land. As with other amphibians, gills change to lungs and fins develop into legs.

In more *arid* climates, southern leopard frogs are often paler in color, a gray or dull green, and spotting is less vivid.

The leopard frog, including all species, is one of the most common amphibians in North America. They can live in brackish marshes along the coast, in deserts, lowlands, or high in the mountains. They are found in springs, creeks, rivers, ponds, canals, and reservoirs where permanent water and aquatic vegetation, such as cattails, grow. When frightened on land, they will look for water and then give a zigzag jump into the safety of the water. This frog can be found at night by its *eyeshine*.

The leopard frog makes a sound similar to a motor boat, along with grunting and chuckling noises that last about one to three seconds. When a number of frogs join together, they sound like a moaning, grunting and chuckling chorus.

13

GAR, spotted

Scientific Name: *Lepisosteus oculatus*
Average Weight: 3 pounds
Average Length: 2¹/₂ feet
Texas Habitat: Coastal fresh and brackish waters, especially near marshes

Gars may be recognized from other fishes by their long, beak-like snouts and sharp teeth. They also have hard, *interlocking,* diamond-shaped scales which cover their long bodies.

Gars are *air breathers.* Because of this, they can live in *stagnant* water in which few other fish can live.

Although gars are considered freshwater fish, they can also live in saltwater and are found in coastal bays and the Gulf of Mexico. Three species of the Gar Family are common in Texas: alligator gar, spotted gar, and longnose gar. Another species, the shortnose gar, is rarer in Texas, but is more commonly found in the fresh waters of Louisiana.

The spotted gar (pictured here) has an olive green body with black spots on fins, head, and sides. It is darker than the other common species of gars. Unlike the alligator gar, the spot-ted gar seldom enters saltwater or the Gulf of Mexico.

Adult gars sometimes travel in *schools,* especially when they spawn. They spawn in early spring and prefer to do so in running water. If this is not available, they will deposit their eggs in shallow water. Gar eggs are a greenish color and are said to be poisonous. Young gar feed on small fish and insects. The adults are mostly fish eaters.

At one time, gars were considered harmful to the fishing industry. Now *environmentalists* realize that they are predators that keep down the population of troublesome *forage* fish. Because gars are fierce fighters when caught on a hook, they are exciting to catch. But gar fishing is not a very popular sport. In southeast Texas and Louisiana, gar meat is considered good to eat and is sold in fish markets.

HARDHEAD catfish

Scientific Name: *Arius felis*
Other Names: Sea catfish, tourist trout, sea cat
Average Weight: 1/2–3 pounds
Average Length: 1–2 feet
Texas Habitat: Shallow bays and harbors along the coast; also coastal freshwater

The hardhead catfish is not a very popular fish. It is frequently caught on a hook and line and is considered a *trash fish*. Also called a "bait stealer," the hardhead is always ready to bite any baited hook and drives more desirable fish away from the bait. Hardhead catfish often live in muddy waters where other fish are scarce. The hardhead is a *scavenger* that eats almost anything it can find, whether dead or alive. They feed in schools along the beaches, in harbors, bays, inlets, and offshore.

This catfish has four barbels under its chin. It has blue or gray sides and white *venters*. The barbels serve as *sensors* to help the hardhead find food as it prowls along the bottom. It has a forked tail and hard, sharp spines in front of the *dorsal* and *pectoral* fins. Care must be taken when handling this fish because the sharp spines can cause painful cuts and the sheaths around the spines are poisonous. Catfish do not have scales; they have smooth skin.

After the female hardhead lays her eggs, the male becomes the caretaker. He carries the eggs in his mouth for about two months. Even after the young fish hatch, the male carries them in his mouth a while longer.

Many species of catfish are warm, freshwater fish, but the hardhead belongs to a species that lives in saltwater and sometimes swims into fresh.

Although some people eat hardheads, the channel catfish, a freshwater fish, is considered a much better food source. Channel cat are raised in commercial hatcheries for this purpose.

ISURUS oxyrinchus (mako shark)

Scientific Name: *Isurus oxyrinchus*
Other Names: Mako shark, mackerel shark, sharp-nosed shark
Average Weight: Heavy; a 10-foot mako shark can weigh as much as 1,000 pounds
Average Length: 6–15 feet
Texas Habitat: Coastal and offshore waters of the Gulf of Mexico

Because no fish or swimming thing could be found whose common name begins with "I," the genus name for shark, *Isurus,* was chosen for this letter. The shark pictured is a mako shark. Its full scientific name is *Isurus oxyrinchus.*

The mako shark belongs to a group called "mackerel" sharks because it is shaped like a mackerel. Because of their fierceness and large size, sharks have always been interesting to people. The number and size of teeth vary in each member of the Shark Family, and this is one way that they can be identified.

The mako shark is capable of making great leaps in and out of the water, especially when trying to free itself when caught on a hook. Fishermen consider it a great sport to try to catch a mako. The slender, beautiful black shark with a white belly is highly prized as a game fish. The meat is said to be delicious.

The skin of a mako shark is made up of tiny scales, which give it a rough, sandpaper-like texture. Makos usually swim near the top of the water, and the tips of their fins can be seen as the powerful swimmer moves along. They eat mackerel, herring, and much larger fish as well. They have large mouths with strong, sharp teeth.

All species of mackerel sharks, including the mako, are large, *voracious* fish. Makos have probably attacked swimmers and even lunged at boats, but it is the great white shark that has the terrible reputation. The white shark is sometimes as long as twenty feet and has been known to eat man-sized seals and other large creatures.

16

JELLYFISH

Scientific Name:	*Physalia physalia*
Other Names:	**Portuguese man-of-war, blue jellyfish**
Average Weight:	**1/2 pound**
Average Length:	**Discs 6–10 inches wide; tentacles may be up to 50 feet long when relaxed**
Texas Habitat:	**Coastal waters**

The Portuguese man-of-war is often called a jellyfish, although it is not a "true" jellyfish. It is distantly related, however, and because it floats and feeds like jellyfish, and is so common in Texas, it is used as our "J."

The Portuguese man-of-war's balloon-like body is filled with gas, which allows it to float and be blown with the wind. True jellyfish move themselves through the water by contractions of the disc or bell. This is like squeezing a half rubber ball back and forth, expelling water with each squeeze and causing jet-like movements. Another difference between a Portuguese man-of-war and a true jellyfish is that the man-of-war is made up of a *colony* of *fused* individuals. A true jellyfish is only one individual.

Most jellyfish, including the Portuguese man-of-war, are shaped like bells or saucers.

Their slender tentacles usually hang down from the edge of the bell. The Portuguese man-of-war has numerous, long tentacles (sometimes as long as fifty feet when the animal is relaxed) that stream out from its sack-like dome. It has been called a "living parachute." The tentacles contain *nematocysts*. These are discharged by the stinging cells to immobilize the jellyfish's prey. The Portuguese man-of-war is bluish-white in color.

All jellyfish can cause discomfort when they strike a person, but the Portuguese man-of-war is one of the most dangerous. One sting by a Portuguese man-of-war can cause great discomfort; if a person is stung by numerous tentacles from a colony, this can be extremely dangerous. Signs are posted at the Padre Island National Seashore when large numbers of this creature are found.

17

KILLIFISH, Gulf

Scientific Name: *Fundulus grandis*
Other Names: Chub, finger mullet
Average Weight: 1 ounce
Average Length: 1–7 inches
Texas Habitat: Saltwater of bays but sometimes enters coastal freshwater

Killifishes are also called "topminnows" because of their habit of eating large quantities of mosquito *larvae* and other insects from the top of the water. They have small, upturned mouths placed close to the tops of their heads and lower protruding jaws, which enable them to forage in this way. Because they eat undesirable larvae and insects, they are beneficial to man. They are also used as bait to catch other fish. Although they are often called "minnows," killifishes are not true minnows. Killifishes have teeth, which true minnows do not have. They also have unforked, rounded tails.

Killifishes often spawn on the beach and deposit their eggs at the time of a new and full moon, when the tides are highest.

There are thirty-six members of the Killifish Family in the United States, but the Gulf killifish is one of the most common in Texas.

In most forms of this species, the young have stripes which fade with age. In some areas, however, the Gulf killifish has dark stripes that remain throughout its life. This species has a broader snout than other species of killifish, but it is sometimes hard to tell one species from another.

Killifishes are common in waters where the amount of salt in the water varies. They can tolerate the largest range of *salinity* of any fish, and they sometimes enter coastal freshwaters.

LING

Scientific Name: *Rachycentron canadus*
Other Names: Cobia, black bonito, lemonfish, coalfish, crab-eater
Average Weight: 15–30 pounds
Average Length: Up to 70 inches
Texas Habitat: Warm coastal waters

The ling is a large fish with a brown back, silvery sides, and a forked tail. It has eight sharp, stout *spines* in front of its rather long dorsal fin. It also has a projecting lower jaw that gives it a mean look. Young lings have black and white stripes which fade with age.

A ling does not act like any other fish and it is the only member of the Cobia Family. Lings are very fast swimmers. This fish will swim under or near floating or stationary objects such as buoys, debris, large fish, and even large turtles. They may even swim under ships and move along with the vessel.

Lings often feed on the bottom, eating crabs, crawfish, and flounders. They also eat some kinds of surface fish. Lings are likely to strike a bait that is trolled or cast near them. Harpoons are also used to catch lings.

Lings are a favorite food and game fish with saltwater *anglers*. They are also caught by commercial fishermen for sale in fish markets.

Not much is known about the life cycle of this fish.

19

MULLET, striped

Scientific Name:	*Mugil cephalus*
Other Names:	**Black mullet, fatback, macho, machuts, lisa, jumper**
Average Weight:	**1/2 to 1 pound (in Laguna Madre, near Padre Island, they may weigh as much as 5 or 6 pounds, sometimes as much as 14 pounds)**
Average Length:	**May be as long as 3 feet, but usually much shorter**
Texas Habitat:	***Temperate* waters of Gulf of Mexico**

Mullets are a type of school fish. They frequent beaches, harbors, bays, and the mouths of rivers. Although striped mullets are considered saltwater fish, they often swim many miles up rivers into freshwater. There are several members of the Mullet Family in Texas, but the striped mullet is the one that is most important to fishermen.

The back of a striped mullet is black or dark blue. The fish has rather large scales. The side scales are arranged so that they give the appearance of stripes. The underside of the fish is a silverish color. Mullets have blunt noses and relatively small mouths.

Because of their acrobatic habit of leaping from the water and plopping back in with a noisy splash, people expect striped mullets to be game fish. However, they usually will not strike a baited hook. Occasionally, they are caught on artificial flies or balls of dough. They put up quite a fight. More often they are caught in *seines*.

Because the small mullets are too full of bones to be good to eat, they are often cut up and used as bait to catch other fish. Mullets caught in Florida are considered delicious. In Texas, they are said to have an oily taste and are not usually eaten.

Mullets swim along the bottom of the water, picking up mud and then straining it through sieve-like gills. They swallow what is edible and spit out what is not. Their food is ground up in their *gizzard*-like stomachs in order to make it digestible.

This fish spawns far offshore and may migrate up all Texas rivers, except where stopped by a dam.

NEWT, black-spotted

Scientific Name: *Notophthalmus meridionalis*
Average Weight: 1/10–2/10 of an ounce
Average Length: 4 1/2 inches
Texas Habitat: Ponds, pools, *resacas* of South Texas, swamps, streams, and moist places out of direct sunlight; the *eft* is found in wooded areas

The newt is a salamander, although it is often called a lizard. No other salamander has the same coloring as the black-spotted newt. On land, it is an orange-red with red spots. In the water, it changes to yellowish-green with red spots.

The skin of this newt is smooth and soft, and it has no gills. There are yellow and black spots on its stomach. The tail is *keeled*.

The black-spotted newt has a pointed snout and prominent *cranial* ridges. It also has three pits on the side of its head and a dark line from the nostril through the eye to the neck.

The larva stage of this creature has gills and lives in the water. From this stage it turns into an eft, which is the name for a young or immature newt. As an eft, it comes out on land for two or three years and then reenters water to become entirely aquatic.

Adult newts are seldom seen by man and are often confused with lizards. They are nocturnal. In the daytime they stay under rocks. At night they crawl around the bottom of ponds and pools in search of food. Their diet consists of insects and other small *invertebrates* and their eggs.

Newts have tails throughout their lifetimes, unlike frogs and toads, which have tails only during their tadpole stages. Newts have no external ears. Also, they never have more than four toes on their unclawed front feet. Lizards (which are not salamanders) usually have five toes on their front feet, and all their toes are clawed. Lizards also have dry, scaly skin. Salamanders breathe by means of gills, or lungs, or through the skin or the inside of the mouth. They can regrow a lost tail or limb. Newts live short lives.

OCTOPUS

Scientific Name: *Octopus vulgaris*
Other Names: Devilfish
Average Weight: 20 pounds
Average Length: 3 feet wide
Texas Habitat: Gulf of Mexico

The octopus is a strange creature with an undeserved bad reputation. The truth is that it is afraid of anything bigger than itself. It has always been the prey of eels, especially the moray, and of man. Although octopuses like to eat fish, they usually feed on crabs and other shellfish because fish are too fast to be caught. An octopus has a parrot-like beak which enables it to break open shells. Octopuses belong to a group of animals called *mollusks*.

Octopuses have eight arms with *suckers* level with the skin. They also have lidless, intelligent-looking eyes that always seem to be staring.

Octopuses come in all sizes — some are only fingernail size, but most are no larger than three feet across. Only in the deep waters of the Pacific Ocean are the really large, movie-type octopuses found.

The octopus can squeeze through an opening that seems much too small for its size. Another special quality of the octopus is its ability to change colors. It has color sacs that enable it to change colors.

To protect itself, the octopus has the ability to eject a dark brown ink. Scientists have not understood exactly what the ink does. It has no effect on the fish that swim through it or upon human skin. The belief of the past was that the ink served as a protective smoke screen. Scientists now believe that it deadens the sense of smell of the moray eel. This keeps the moray from recognizing the octopus as its prey.

Octopuses supposedly can be easily tamed and trained to take food from the hand of an attendant or visitor. They show other signs of intelligence too.

PORPOISE

Scientific Name:	*Tursiops truncatus*
Other Names:	**Bottle-nosed dolphin**
Average Weight:	**May weigh as much as 1,400 pounds**
Average Length:	**9–12 feet**
Texas Habitat:	**Gulf of Mexico**

A study of this animal can be confusing because the names "porpoise" and "dolphin" are both common names used for a group of small whales. We chose "porpoise" so it could be our "P" word. The species pictured is also called a "bottle-nosed dolphin." The bottle-nosed dolphin has a longer snout (about three inches more) than the common porpoise.

Although the porpoise lives in water, it is not a fish. It is an air-breathing *mammal*. The porpoise is actually a small whale, and there are twenty species of these little giants.

Because of a flexible body construction, the porpoise moves with the rhythm of the water, enabling it to swim at great speeds.

Porpoises can be fierce fighters when they must defend their young. They will form a circle around an enemy, such as a shark, and take turns ramming the shark with their heads to either drive it away or kill it. These animals also have the unusual ability to herd other fish and are known as the "cowboys of the sea."

The porpoise has a gray body with a whitish belly. It has a mouth that always seems to be laughing. Born with no teeth, the porpoise develops forty-four to fifty teeth in each jaw within a few weeks after birth. Its flattened tail is notched in the middle, and each side of the tail is called a "fluke." There are two paddle-like limbs near the front of the body.

A porpoise may live to be thirty years old. During its life it is in constant motion, taking naps of thirty seconds to five minutes from time to time. It can stay under water for six minutes without coming up for air.

QUEEN ANGELFISH

Scientific Name: *Holacanthus ciliaris*
Other Names: Angel
Average Weight: 3 pounds
Average Length: Up to 12 inches
Texas Habitat: Deep, warm waters near offshore reefs of the Gulf of Mexico

Members of the Angelfish Family are among the prettiest and most colorful fish. The queen angelfish is one of the largest of this group. It may reach a length of eighteen inches but is usually smaller.

Although this fish may be found in Texas waters, you are more likely to find one in an aquarium or in a store where aquarium supplies are sold. Because it is so colorful and unusual, it makes a beautiful addition to an aquarium. If you visited an island in the Caribbean, you might find this fish in the shallow waters. In Texas you might see it if you went scuba diving in the deep waters near offshore reefs in the Gulf of Mexico.

There are several members of the Angelfish Family, and all are prized as aquarium residents. They all have very different color patterns. Other species found in Texas include the rock beauty and the blue angelfish.

The body of the queen angelfish in its adult stage is purplish-blue and the scales are edged in yellow-orange. The head above the eye is dark blue; below, greenish-yellow. The fins are varying shades of yellow and orange. The entire fish is edged in light blue. Young fish in this species have three light blue stripes on the body and two on the head, as well as a dark band through the eye. The colors of this fish are so bright that it looks as though it has been painted with a brush. As with some other species, the colors and patterns of the queen change as the juvenile fish becomes an adult.

The queen angelfish has a small mouth and small teeth. It feeds on baby crabs, barnacles, and other small invertebrates.

RIBBONFISH

Scientific Name: *Trichiurus lepturus*
Other Names: Atlantic cutlassfish, scabbardfish
Average Weight: 1–2 pounds
Average Length: 4–28 inches, but may be as long as 5 feet
Texas Habitat: Mudflats of the Gulf of Mexico (inshore) and bays

The ribbonfish merits its name because it has a long, silvery body that looks like a ribbon. Because of its snake-like appearance, it is sometimes mistaken for an eel. The eyes and mouth of the ribbonfish are large. The upper jaw, with four fang-like teeth, gives it a fierce look. The lower jaw projects beyond the upper jaw. The dorsal fin begins just behind the head and continues to the tail.

The ribbonfish, which belongs to the Cutlassfish Family, is common near the shore of the Gulf of Mexico. It is frequently caught on a hook and line, particularly at night, when it feeds near the surface of the water. The fish will strike at any baited hook and is considered a "bait stealer." Small ribbonfish are used for bait to catch kingfish. The larger ribbonfish will gobble up a hooked fish before it can be landed. Because of its large teeth, care must be taken to remove a hook from a ribbonfish's mouth.

Ribbonfish die very quickly when brought onto land. In some parts of the world, such as the Orient and the Caribbean, they are considered edible and said to be delicious. However, they are not usually eaten in the United States.

STINGAREE

Scientific Name: *Dasytis sabina*
Other Names: Atlantic stingray
Average Weight: Female 1.3–1.6 pounds; male 1.1 pounds
Average Length: 6–8 inches, but may be as long as 1 foot
Texas Habitat: Bays in the summer, Gulf of Mexico in winter; also the mouths of rivers and sometimes freshwater

The stingaree, which looks like a gray-brown saucer with a pointed head on one side and a long whip-like tail on the other, is the most common member of the Stingray Family in Texas waters. It spends its winters in the Gulf of Mexico, *migrates* to the bays in summer, and can be found in the mouths of rivers, entering into freshwater from time to time.

Stingarees do not look as though they have fins, but they do. They have a large pectoral fin on each side, which they flap in order to swim. Their gill slits, five on each side, are located under their bodies. The mouth is also on the underside of the body. The eyes and *spiracles* are on the topside.

Stingarees often come into beach areas and can be very troublesome to swimmers. The tail, covered with small, prickly spines, causes a painful, stinging sensation if it strikes.

Stingarees live on or near the bottom of the water and feed on worms, mollusks, and crustaceans. They eat both animal and vegetable matter, which means that they are *omnivorous*. Stingarees make their beds in the sand of shallow water and can be *gigged* like flounders. Although stingarees do not look very tasty, they are considered edible.

Another member of the Stingray Family that looks much like the stingaree is the southern stingray. It grows much larger than the stingaree (sometimes as wide as five feet) and has a long, dangerous spine. More people are hurt by these stingrays and the Portuguese man-of-war than any other coastal animals.

Skates, sawfish, and guitarfish are related to stingrays. They all have flattened bodies and large side fins, but they are not all as flat as a stingaree.

26

TURTLE, snapping

Scientific Name: *Chelydra serpentina*
Other Names: **Snapper**
Average Weight: **Up to 50 pounds**
Average Length: **Up to 17 inches**
Texas Habitat: **Any kind of freshwater, preferably that which is muddy**

The snapping turtle is one of the largest freshwater turtles in Texas. Turtles have a shell or *carapace*, which has ridges. They also have *warts* on the neck and legs. The eyes of the snapping turtle can be seen from directly above.

Snapping turtles will prowl on land and are sometimes seen near homes and towns. Turtles are often struck and killed by cars when they walk onto a road or highway.

This turtle got its name because of the way it "snaps" up its food. When it sees something that looks good to eat, it will lie in wait, then snap up its prey with a quick lunge. The snapping turtle eats plants, crayfish, fish, clams, frogs, salamanders, and even dead and decaying matter, called *carrion*.

Turtles live long lives. Some have been known to live as long as twenty years. The snapping turtle is considered a good food source and is used to make soup.

Turtles are interesting to study because their ancestry goes back millions of years. There has been little change in appearance in all that time. They do, however, adapt to their environment. Although all turtles have four limbs, some have feet, webs, or flippers — depending on where they live. There are 250 species of turtles worldwide, divided into twelve families. In North America, there are thirty-eight species belonging to seven families.

A turtle is really a reptile with a shell. They are air breathers and have lungs. The body of an aquatic turtle is built in such a way that it can stay under water for a long time.

Although most turtles are silent, some make hissing, barking, or grunting sounds. They are among the most intelligent of the reptiles.

URCHIN, sea

Scientific Name: *Lytechinus variegatus*
Other Names: Living pincushion
Average Weight: 1–2 ounces
Average Width: 1 1/2–10 inches
Texas Habitat: Shallow water of the Gulf of Mexico

A sea urchin, when it is alive, looks like a pincushion full of pins. When found on the shore after it dies, it looks like a hollow doorknob covered with decorations.

The ball-like creature is covered with short, movable spines which are thin tubes. Each spine ends in a sucker. These suckers serve as feet and enable the urchin to pull itself along on rocks or the bottom of the water.

In Texas, this species of sea urchin is found mostly in grassbeds of shallow water in bays near the Gulf of Mexico. Sometimes as many as fifteen adults will gather in a small area. They are preyed upon by birds and mollusks, but because of the spines, the urchin is not easily harmed (except at its mouth, which is located at the base of its shell). Urchins live on *organic* matter, including small animals and waste ma-terial.

The sea urchin will cover the upper part of its spiny body with bits of seagrass or shell. Supposedly, this is done to protect the urchin from the rays of the sun in the shallow waters where they live. Although it is not known for certain, sea urchins are believed to live for two or three years.

This species of sea urchin has many color variations. The *test* (skeleton) may be purple, green, red, or mottled with white. Even the color of spines will vary. They can be purple, green, red, or white at the tip of the spine and another color at the base. The colors change with environmental conditions. Some urchins are brown, as is the one pictured.

This creature is considered edible in Europe and the Orient.

VOLADOR

Scientific Name:	*Istiophorus americanus*
Other Names:	**Atlantic sailfish, Aguja prieta, sail, spearfish, spikefish**
Average Weight:	**30–40 pounds**
Average Length:	**5 feet**
Texas Habitat:	**Deep waters of the Gulf of Mexico**

Volador is a Spanish name for the Atlantic sailfish. It is easy to understand why the volador is called a sailfish. It has a dorsal fin, which extends from just behind the head to the forked tail and spreads open like a spiny sail. The volador belongs to a group of fish called "spearfish" because of their long, spear-like beaks.

Voladors are dark blue with rows of black dots between the spines. The spots become less noticeable when the mood of the fish changes. The "sail" fin has *rays* or spokes like an umbrella. The spokes allow the fin to fold down into a groove along the back when the fish goes under water. In this position it cannot be seen. The fins are paper-thin, bluish-green or bluish-purple. The lower half of the fish fades to white.

This fish uses its long, slender, sharp bill to attack its prey. Like all fish that have bills or spears, the sailfish has no teeth.

The volador lives far offshore in deep waters and is called a "blue water" fish. It is considered a prize catch for fishermen and is caught by *trolling* cut bait or *feather jigs* near places where the fish might be.

The fish spawns in late spring and early summer in shallow waters of Florida. The larvae then float northward into the Gulf Stream and offshore in the Gulf of Mexico. It is said that one female may spawn as many as 4,675,000 eggs, but most of the larvae are eaten by other fish.

After the eggs hatch, baby sailfish begin to eat tiny shrimp-like creatures called "copepods." As the volador grows, it eats small mollusks and then little fish. After only a year, sailfish reach a length of five or six feet and are soon sought after by sport fishermen.

WHITING, Gulf

Scientific Name:	*Menticirrhus littoralis*
Other Names:	Carolina whiting, sand whiting, silver whiting, Gulf kingfish, sea mullet, shoemaker
Average Weight:	1¹/₂–2 pounds
Average Length:	1 foot
Texas Habitat:	Near sandy beaches of the Gulf Coast; saltwater

The Gulf whiting looks like a streak of silver as it swims through the water. The back of this fish is a dusky silver; the sides are bright silver, and the underside is almost white. It is often confused with southern king-whiting, which has blotches along its sides.

The Gulf whiting belongs to the Croaker Family, which has more members than any other fish family in Texas. The family is so named because of the croaking sounds that its members make.

Gulf whiting are good to eat and are caught all during the year in Texas. Shrimp is the best bait to use when fishing for Gulf whiting.

This fish feeds along the bottom on small crabs, mollusks, shrimp, and small fish. Gulf whiting are fast-growing, short-lived fish. They spawn in the shallow waters of the Gulf of Mexico. After hatching, the larvae spend the first summer of their lives in the ocean surf. As little fish, they swim back into the deeper waters of the Gulf of Mexico.

Whitings are often listed in textbooks as kingfish. Either name can be used.

XIPHIAS gladius

Other Names:	Swordfish
Average Weight:	100–400 pounds, but may weigh up to 1/2 ton
Average Length:	13–15 feet
Texas Habitat:	Cold, deep waters of the Gulf of Mexico

No fish with a common name begins with "X," so we have used *Xiphias,* the genus name for swordfish. The full scientific name is *Xiphias gladius.*

Swordfish are highly prized as a food fish, and when one is caught far out in the Gulf of Mexico, it is usually cut up and put into cold storage for the trip back to shore. For this reason, it was difficult to find a photograph of this fish.

It is easy to understand why the *Xiphias* was given the common name of swordfish. It has a long snout and the upper jaw extends into a long, pointed "sword," which is one-third as long as the fish's body. A six-foot swordfish will have a bill or "sword" that is two feet long. It uses its bill to stun or impale the fish that it eats. The favorite food of the swordfish is mackerel.

This fish has been known to spear the side of a wooden ship. There is even a record of a swordfish having speared the side of a research submarine. Swordfish have no scales or teeth. The back and sides of this fish are a dark bronze color. The lower sides and belly are gray, and the fins are dark.

The swordfish is a very fast swimmer, timed at speeds as high as sixty miles an hour. It is considered a great game fish and puts up quite a fight when hooked. Because it has a soft, delicate mouth, the hook can be torn out and the fish will swim free. Great fishing skill is required to land a swordfish which will leap, dive, and swim rapidly in its struggle to get away. Very strong tackle is required to catch the *Xiphias.* Landing one may take several hours.

Swordfish steaks are often listed on restaurant menus. The fish is harvested commercially by harpooning or on a long line.

31

YELLOWFIN tuna

Scientific Name: *Thunnus albacares*
Other Names: Alantic yellowfin tuna, tunny
Average Weight: 100 pounds
Average Length: 8 feet
Texas Habitat: Gulf of Mexico and other warm, saltwater areas

The yellowfin tuna lives in warm, tropical waters around the world. In Texas it is found in the Gulf of Mexico near Port Isabel. The tuna can be caught with rod and reel and is highly prized as a game fish. It is also caught commercially in seines and is considered the most valuable food fish in the United States.

The next time you eat a tuna sandwich, remember the yellowfin. This fish has been caught so widely that its numbers are growing smaller. Scientists are trying to find a species that can be used as a substitute food source to allow the yellowfin population to increase.

The yellowfin tuna has a tremendous appetite and gobbles up flying fish, sardines, squid, and other small fish. It eats so much that it has been known to gain as much as sixty pounds in one year. Yellowfins swim in schools, as do most other members of the Mackerel Family.

This fish is called a yellowfin because of the yellowish color on its fins. The breast also has a yellow tint. The back of the fish is dark blue shading to silver on the lower half. The dorsal fin, as well as the anal fin, is extremely long and sometimes reaches all the way back to the forked tail. All members of the Mackerel Family have forked tails.

ZOSTERAE, Hippocampus

Scientific Name:	*Hippocampus zosterae*
Other Names:	**Dwarf seahorse, pygmy seahorse**
Average Weight:	**1/10 ounce**
Average Length:	**2–8 inches**
Texas Habitat:	**Gulf waters, shallow seas, and estuaries (prefer high salinity and grass flats)**

No swimming thing with a common name beginning with "Z" could be found, so we have used *zosterae*. This is the species name for dwarf seahorse.

Seahorses are not always recognized as fish because they do not look like any other fish. Some seahorses live in shallow water, where they are often caught in shrimp *trawlers*.

This is the smallest member of the Seahorse Family, sometimes less than two inches long. Larger species are seven to eight inches long. Seahorses have long bodies, a curled tail, a tube-like snout, and hard scales that serve as a protective armor.

No other fish swims in an upright position as though standing up as the seahorse does. They propel themselves through the water by rapidly moving the dorsal fin.

The birth process of seahorses is very unusual. After the female lays her eggs, she deposits them in a brood *pouch,* which is a part of the male's body. The embryos are nurtured in the pouch for about ten days until the babies emerge. The father gives jerking motions as the babies come into the world, usually one at a time. There may be as many as twenty *zosterae* babies from one pouch, and the process takes several hours. The babies look like miniature adult seahorses.

The tiny, thin babies drift for a few moments, then begin to swim upright and wrap their little tails around nearby vegetation. Baby seahorses grow quickly and mature within a few months.

The *zosterae,* or dwarf seahorse, is commonly found in grassbeds along with sea urchins.

Glossary

Many of these words have other meanings. We have used only those definitions that apply to the subjects of this book.

air breather: Something that requires breathing air to live.

amphibian: A creature that can live on land or in water. These creatures usually lay eggs as a means of reproduction.

anal fin: The fin on the underside of the body near the tail.

angler: One who fishes with hook and line.

antenna: One of a pair of long, slender sensory organs, as on a crab or insect. (Antennae is plural form.)

aquatic: That which lives in the water.

arid: Dry; parched with heat.

barbel: Soft, threadlike appendage to the jaws or chin or nostrils of certain fishes, used as an organ of touch and taste.

bay: A part of sea or lake indenting the shoreline.

berried: Carrying eggs on the outside of the body like a large mass of tiny berries.

brackish: Somewhat salty.

carapace: Hard, bony outer case or covering of a creature such as a crab, turtle, or lobster.

carrion: Dead and decaying flesh.

colony: A group of individuals of the same species living together for mutual benefit. They may be structurally united (as in the Portuguese man-of-war) or separate. They may be alike in form or of different types.

contract: To draw together.

cranial: Pertaining to the skull.

crayfish: A small freshwater crustacean somewhat resembling a small lobster.

crustacean: Having a crust or hard shell. Refers to a class of invertebrates, including shrimps, crabs, barnacles, and lobsters, which usually live in the water and breathe through gills; they have hard shells and jointed appendages and bodies.

decapod: Ten-footed or ten-armed; any ten-legged crustacean.

dorsal fin: Dorsal refers to the back, thus a dorsal fin is one along the back.

eft: Immature newt.

environmentalist: One who works to protect the environment.

estuary: An area where fresh water meets salt water. The water is usually brackish.

eyeshine: Reflection of light shown in the eye of an animal, such as a frog.

feather-jig: A leaded hook skirted with feathers instead of bait.

fertilize: To make fertile or productive; to begin the process of reproduction.

fin: Winglike organ on the body of a fish; structure with membranes supported by soft rays or spines.

forage: To search for food.

fry: Recently hatched fish; also, very small adult fish.

fuse: To join as if by melting.

game fish: A fish caught for sport.

genus: A grouping or category of plants and animals ranking next above the species and next below the family. The genus name is always capitalized and in italics and precedes the species name, which is not capitalized but is also in italics. Example: *Alligator mississippiensis.*

gigged: To be caught with a fish spear, usually on the bottom.

gills: The organ for breathing for most animals that live in the water (fish, lobsters, etc.).

gizzard: An intestinal organ that grinds up food so that it can be digested by the stomach.

hatchery: A place where fish or other animals that lay eggs are kept for reproduction.

ichthyology: The study of fish.

incubate: To sit upon eggs to hatch them; to keep eggs in favorable condition for hatching.

interlocking: Joining things together firmly, especially by hooking, dovetailing, or twisting.

invertebrate: An animal that lacks a spinal column.

keeled: Shaped like a ship's keel.

larva: The wingless, often wormlike form in which insects hatch from the egg; also, the earliest form of a young animal (as a tadpole) that is fundamentally unlike its parent. (Larvae is plural form.)

mammal: An animal which secretes milk to nourish its young.

median fin: Fin that is located near the middle.

migrate: To move from one place to another.

mollusk: A large group of mostly shelled and aquatic invertebrate animals, including snails, clams, oysters, and squid.

molt: To shed skin or shell, especially when it will be replaced by new growth.

mottled: Marked with blotches or spots of different colors or shades.

native: Occurring naturally in a particular place; does not need to be imported.

nematocyst: A structure discharged by the stinging cells of a Portuguese man-of-war or jellyfish.

nocturnal: Active at night.

omnivorous: Feeds on both animal and vegetable matter.

organic: Natural material, such as vegetation.

pectoral fin: A fin located on the breast or chest area.

pincer: A claw resembling pliers, like those of a crab or lobster.

pouch: A small bag or sack.

predator: A creature that hunts other creatures for food.

ray: Any support of a fin.

reef: A ridge of rocks or sand at or near the surface of the water.

reptile: Any of a class of cold-blooded, air-breathing vertebrates (including snakes, crocodiles, lizards, and turtles) having hard skeletons and bodies usually covered with horny plates or scales.

resacas: A pond-like body of water found in South Texas which resembles a bayou. It has an outlet to another body of water (such as the Rio Grande) and the water flows in and out. Resacas is a Spanish word meaning "flowing."

salinity: Containing salt.

scales: A small, bony plate in the skin occurring in varying shapes and compositions.

scavenger: Something that eats anything, even that which is considered trash.

school: A large number of fish or water animals of the same kind swimming together.

scientific name: Made up of a genus name, which always begins with a capital, and a species name that is lowercased. These words are always in italics. They are almost always Latin names, which are very difficult to pronounce but are descriptive and help explain characteristics of the object.

seine: A large, weighted fishing net.

sensor: An organ or device that responds to a physical stimulus.

snout: The forward projecting part of an animal's head.

spawn: (verb) To produce or deposit eggs.
(noun) The mass of eggs emitted by fishes.

species: A category of animals or plants. Also defined as a natural unit of animals in which interbreeding occurs.

spine: A bone-like support of a fin.

spiracle: The opening behind the eye in some fishes (like stingrays) connecting with the gill cavity for pumping water.

stagnant: Without motion or current; not flowing or moving.

submerge: To place or plunge under water.

subtropical: Refers to areas adjacent to tropical regions.

sucker: A part of an animal's body used for sucking or clinging.

swim bladder: A sac-like organ filled with air that keeps an animal afloat.

tadpole: The aquatic larva of an amphibian, such as a frog or toad, breathing by external gills and having a tail which gives it a fish-like form. Also called polliwog.

temperate: Not hot or cold; moderate.

test: The skeleton of a sea urchin or a sand dollar.

trash fish: A fish that is not good to eat or to use as bait or for any other purpose; one that is thrown away when caught.

trawler: One who uses a trawl, or a stout fishing line with many lines and baitless hooks; also, a large fishing net shaped like a flattened bag which is pulled behind the boat.

troll: To fish by pulling a hook and line through the water.

venters: The undersurface of the abdomen of invertebrates.

vertebrate: An animal that has a spinal column.

voracious: Eating with greediness.

wart: A small, horny projection or bump on the skin.

zoology: The study of animals.

Illustration Credits

All photographs for this book were taken by Dr. H. Dickson Hoese of the University of Southwestern Louisiana, with the exception of the "X" (swordfish) which was taken by George Grimmer, Jr. We wish to acknowledge those institutions that allowed the use of their locations, aquariums, or mounted specimens. The animals not included on this list were photographed by Dr. Hoese in their natural habitat.

Alligator, full:	Houston Zoo
Bass:	Hot Springs National Park Aquarium
Drum, black:	Sea-Arama Marine World, Galveston, Texas
Eel:	University of Texas Marine Laboratory, Port Aransas, Texas
Jellyfish (Portuguese man-of-war):	Padre Island National Seashore
Newt:	Brownsville Zoo
Octopus:	Pan American Marine Laboratory, South Padre Island
Porpoise:	Sea-Arama Marine World, Galveston, Texas
Queen angelfish:	Houston Museum of Natural History
Turtle:	Courtesy Dan Holland, University of Southwestern Louisiana
Volador (sailfish):	Blessing Hotel, Blessing, Texas
Whiting:	Padre Island National Seashore

We also appreciate the help of many other individuals and institutions, including John Brundrett, taxidermist, Port Aransas; Audubon Park Zoo, New Orleans; Texas Parks and Wildlife Department; and the Louisiana Department of Wildlife and Fisheries.

Bibliography

To write a book about twenty-six "things" that swim in Texas waters required information from many sources. It was like going on a treasure hunt and finding a little bit here and a little bit there. The following texts were my primary sources of information.

Beachcomber's Guide to Gulf Coast Marine Life, by Nick Fotheringham. Houston: Gulf Publishing Company, 1980.

Complete Field Guide to American Wildlife, by Henry Hill Collins, Jr. New York: Harper and Row, 1959.

Fieldbook of Natural History, by E. Laurence Palmer. McGraw-Hill, 1975.

Field Guide to Western Reptiles and Amphibians, A, by Robert C. Stebbins. Boston: Houghton Mifflin Company, 1966.

Fishes of the Gulf of Mexico, by H. Dickson Hoese and Richard H. Moore. College Station: Texas A & M Press, 1977.

Food and Game Fishes of the Texas Coast, compiled by Patricia Pew. Austin: Texas Parks and Wildlife Department, 1971.

Fresh and Salt Water Fishes of the World, The, by Edward C. Migdalski and George S. Fichter. New York: Alfred A. Knopf, 1976.

Freshwater Fishes of Texas, by Robert J. Kemp, Jr. Bulletin 5-A, Texas Parks and Wildlife Department, Austin, Texas, 1971.

North American Wildlife, by Durward L. Allen, editor. Pleasantville, NY: Reader's Digest, 1982.

Oxford Book of Vertebrates, The, by Marion Nixon and Derek Whiteley. Oxford University Press, 1972.

Seashores. New York: Golden Press, 1985.

Wondrous World of Fishes. Washington, DC: National Geographic Society, 1965.